DOES AI SCARE YOU?

Yes. No. Maybe.

Mark Anderson, PhD

Selection. Intention. Restraint. Alignment. Purpose.

Copyright

Mark Anderson, PhD
18 Dover Street Suite 492
Norwell, Massachusetts 02061

First edition
Printed in the United States

ISBN 978-0-9997340-9-4 (ebook)
ISBN 979-8-9949357-0-5 (print)

Disclaimer

This book is provided for informational and educational purposes only. The author and publisher make no representations or warranties regarding the accuracy, completeness, or suitability of the information contained in this book for any purpose.

The author and publisher expressly disclaim any responsibility or liability for any loss, injury, adverse effects, or damages—direct or indirect—that may result from the use or application of any information, suggestions, or ideas presented in this book. Readers assume full responsibility for how they choose to use the information contained herein.

All product names, trademarks, and registered trademarks mentioned in this book are the property of their respective owners and are used for identification and educational purposes only. No endorsement is implied. Any products mentioned are used solely as illustrative examples as nominative fair use.

The ideas in this book represent the author's perspective at the time of writing. Because both artificial intelligence and human understanding continue to evolve, these views may change over time.

Acknowledgements

This book grew out of many conversations — with colleagues, students, and friends — who were willing to admit uncertainty in a world that rewards confidence.

I am grateful to those who asked difficult questions, challenged easy assumptions, and reminded me that thinking remains a human responsibility.

No machines were harmed in the writing of this book.
Several habits and choices were examined.

This book exists because of curiosity, good conversations, judgment, purpose, and the quiet patience of people who allowed important ideas to evolve.

Dedication

This book is dedicated to everyone who has ever tried to understand if — and how — artificial intelligence (AI) impacts their lives.

To everyone who has ever wondered
what it means to live alongside intelligent machines.

For those who still pause
before accepting an answer.

A Note on Reading This Book

This book is written a little differently on purpose.

You may notice short lines.
Intentional pauses.
Fragments.

Ellipses.
Em dashes.
White space.

This is not a formatting mistake.
It is part of the experience.

The subject of this book is attention, intention, and thoughtful decision-making in the age of artificial intelligence. The writing style mirrors that theme by encouraging moments of pause and reflection.

Some ideas are meant to land quickly.
Others are meant to linger.

You are not meant to rush through these pages.
You are meant to notice your own thoughts while reading them.

If you find yourself slowing down, rereading a sentence, or pausing between paragraphs — the book is working exactly as intended.

That quiet moment of awareness — the instant you step back and observe your own thinking — is where the most important conversations in this book truly begin.

It is the part of the mind — often associated with the brain's anterior prefrontal cortex — that reflects, imagines, evaluates, and chooses with intention. This book is designed to invite that part of you into the conversation.

Table of Contents

Preface

Before You Ask the Machine

No one wakes up in the morning hoping to become obsolete.
That may sound blunt, but it captures a quiet anxiety of our time.

Yet we find ourselves living in a moment when machines can write essays, summarize books we have not read, generate art we did not practice for, and answer questions we did not fully think through.

Artificial Intelligence (AI) arrived not with a single dramatic announcement, but as evolving tools and through quiet convenience. It became part of our workflows, inboxes, phones, media, movies — and eventually, into our conversations. Then, it became a topic everyone was talking about.

That alone does not make it dangerous.
It does make it powerful.
It offers possibilities.

This book is not about fearing AI and autonomous machines. If fear alone were useful, human history would look very different. Printing presses were once accused of destroying memory. Calculators were said to rot the mind. The internet was predicted to end thinking and deep thought forever — a claim that, depending on the day, may still be under evaluation.

AI belongs to that lineage of tools. Yet it is different in one important way: not because it thinks, but because it sounds as though it does.

But what really is AI?

Ask friends, teachers, and experts. The answers may surprise you. At its core, modern artificial intelligence is not a digital mind or a synthetic person. It is mathematics applied to enormous amounts of data — patterns, probabilities, and statistics at scale. **The results can become words, images, music, decisions, animations, and art — outputs that feel creative even though they begin as computation.**

Most AI systems learn by studying vast collections of human-created material — language, images, code, decisions, and records of the world. From this data, they learn patterns about what tends to come next: the next word in a sentence, the next pixel in an image, the next likely outcome in a sequence.

When an AI writes a paragraph, it is not recalling a memory or expressing an opinion. It is calculating which words are statistically most likely to follow the previous ones, based on patterns learned during training. The result can feel strikingly human because human language is the very material it was trained on.

This is why AI can appear confident even when it is wrong.
Probability is not understanding.
Fluency is not comprehension.
Prediction is not judgment.

Yet these systems are undeniably useful. They can sift through information faster than any person, identify patterns across massive datasets, and assist with tasks that would otherwise take days or months. In that sense, artificial intelligence is not a betrayal of human intelligence; it is a continuation of it — a tool built by human minds to extend their reach.

A system that speaks fluently, confidently, and instantly invites trust. Sometimes that trust is earned. Sometimes it is simply efficient. The greater risk is not that artificial intelligence replaces humans outright, but that it replaces small acts of judgment so gradually that we stop noticing when we may have ceased practicing them ourselves.

That is where this book begins.

You will not find technical manuals here, nor instructions on how to optimize prompts. There are many excellent resources for that. Instead, this is a book about pauses — the moment before accepting an answer, the moment before delegating a decision, the moment before deciding whether speed is worth the cost.

The title asks a simple question: **Does AI scare you?**

The honest answers are usually just as simple: yes, no, or maybe.

If your answer is yes, that does not make you resistant to progress. It may mean you appreciate the value of caution.
If your answer is no, that does not make you naïve. It may mean you see

opportunity clearly.

And if your answer is maybe, you are not undecided — you are attentive.

Throughout this book, these three positions will reappear, sometimes explicitly, often implicitly. They are not conclusions. They are perspectives. You may move between them. You should.

There are moments of seriousness here, because the stakes are real. Ethics do not emerge automatically from intelligence, artificial or otherwise. They require people willing to think when thinking would be easier to outsource. There are also moments of restraint and humor, because taking ourselves too seriously has never improved judgment — and because humans, unlike machines, occasionally benefit from recognizing their own habits.

The question, then, is not whether machines should think for us, but how much thinking we are willing to stop doing ourselves. Tools designed to extend cognition should not quietly replace it. When they do, the problem is no longer technological. It is human.

If you finish this book with stronger opinions, that is fine.

If you finish it with better questions, that is better still.

Tools themselves are neither good nor evil — they amplify what we bring to them.

The machine can help.

The thinking remains ours.

And the choices ahead will always come back to five human choices: **Selection. Intention. Restraint. Alignment. Purpose.**

Author's Intent

Artificial intelligence is powerful. That much is no longer in question. It is also a remarkable opportunity. What remains uncertain is how we choose to use it—and what we allow it to replace: repetitive tasks, data analysis, and increasingly, thinking itself.

Artificial intelligence uses data-driven algorithms and neural networks to help machines learn patterns, reason, and make decisions through an iterative training process.

This book was written for people who feel both curiosity and a measure of unease—those who see AI's potential to amplify human intelligence and even extend our reach beyond the stars, but who also recognize the risk of outsourcing judgment, ethics, and responsibility.

Does AI Scare You? is not an argument for fear, nor a celebration of blind adoption. It is an invitation to think carefully, independently, and ethically about how we live alongside machines that can mimic intelligence but cannot assume human responsibility.

The questions *Yes. No. Maybe.* are not answers to be memorized; they are positions we may move through as we learn, reflect, and choose how much of our own minds we are willing to keep engaged.

Like all technologies throughout history, artificial intelligence can be used to improve human life or deepen conflict. That choice, now as always, remains entirely human.

Tools have always redistributed effort. They move work from one domain to another. When calculators became common, arithmetic shifted from mental labor to conceptual understanding. When search engines emerged, recall gave way to navigation. Each transition demanded adaptation, not retreat.

Used thoughtfully, AI can enhance human capability rather than diminish it. Machine learning systems can surface patterns humans would never notice unaided. Computer vision can detect anomalies invisible to the naked eye. Language models can synthesize information faster than any single reader could manage. These are not trivial gains. In medicine, science, safety, and accessibility, they matter.

History suggests that equilibrium eventually returns. New skills emerge. New norms form. Responsibility is renegotiated. What feels destabilizing at first becomes mundane. The printing press did not end thought; it changed literacy. The internet did not erase knowledge; it reorganized it.

The Evolution from Computers to AI

1940s–1950s — Early Computers
Machines performed fixed calculations and followed explicit instructions.

1950 — Alan Turing publishes *Computing Machinery and Intelligence*, introducing the Turing Test as a way to discuss machine intelligence.

1950s–1980s — Rule-Based AI

Systems used hand-written "if–then" logic to simulate reasoning.
The field of Artificial Intelligence formally began in 1956 at Dartmouth College, where researchers gathered for the first conference dedicated to what they called "Artificial Intelligence" (cf. **John McCarthy**).

1990s–2010s — Machine Learning Era

AI shifted from programmed rules to learning patterns from data.
Python, the programming language that now powers much of modern AI, was first released to the public in 1991 by Guido van Rossum. Its simplicity and openness helped accelerate the growth of machine learning and AI research decades later. Python continues to develop.
Neural network breakthroughs (2006-2012).

2010s–Present — Deep Learning Breakthrough

Multi-layer neural networks enabled speech recognition, image analysis, and language understanding.
Python became a dominant language for AI and machine learning due to libraries like NumPy, TensorFlow, PyTorch, and scikit-learn.

The deep learning surge of the 2010s was made possible not only by better algorithms, but by advances in specialized hardware (GPUs and TPUs) and the rise of cloud computing that enabled large models to be trained at scale.

2020s–Present — Generative AI

AI systems began creating text, images, music, and code by learning from vast datasets.

The evolution of AI has been gradual: from machines that followed fixed instructions, to systems that learn, adapt, and now generate. When we understand that progression, we are better equipped to choose how we use these tools—with intention, restraint, alignment, and purpose.

How AI Already Shows Up in Daily Life

Most people already interact with AI dozens of times each day without noticing.

- **Smart Assistants**
  Voice tools like Alexa (Amazon) and Siri (Apple) respond to questions, set reminders, and control home devices.

- **Navigation & Traffic Updates**
  Maps adjust routes in real time based on live traffic patterns.

- **Streaming & Shopping Recommendations**
  Platforms suggest music, movies, and products based on past behavior.

- **Spam & Fraud Detection**
  Email filters and banks flag suspicious activity automatically.

- **Customer Support Chatbots**
  Many websites now provide instant, AI-assisted responses.

- **Driver Assistance Features**
  Lane warnings, adaptive cruise control, and parking assistance rely on AI systems.

Tools have always changed us.

What matters is whether we respond with intention, restraint, alignment, and purpose.

For the critical reader: these are not the only human choices that matter. They are the ones this book chooses to explore.

These ideas can be understood as five simple human choices that guide how we use any powerful tool:
Selection — choosing among options
Intention — deciding direction or purpose
Restraint — choosing what not to do
Alignment — choosing consistency with values
Purpose — choosing why something is done

These are not technical skills. They are human ones. And as technology becomes more capable, they become more important, not less.

Thinking is active.

AI amplifies it.

Purpose directs it.

Chapter 1: The Question We Avoid Asking Clearly

We tend to ask the wrong questions about artificial intelligence.

We ask what it can do.
We ask how fast it will improve.
We ask who will win, who will lose, and whether our jobs will still exist in five years.

All of those questions matter.
None of them come first.

The more important question is quieter — and a little uncomfortable:

What are we giving up when we stop thinking for ourselves?

Thinking is not passive consumption. It is deliberate engagement. Artificial intelligence can accelerate thought, but it cannot replace it. The question is not whether AI can think. It is whether we will continue to.

Artificial intelligence did not appear because humans became lazy. It appeared because the world became large — too large for any one mind to hold. Data expanded faster than comprehension. Systems grew more complex than intuition alone could manage. We responded the way we always have: by building tools.

At first, the tools were humble.
Calculations.
Sorting.
Pattern recognition.

Then they became fluent.
They began to explain themselves.
They began to sound confident.

That is where the shift happened.

When a machine produces an answer that sounds thoughtful, it tempts us to skip the thinking that normally comes before agreement. Not because we are careless, but because we are busy. Speed feels like competence. Confidence feels like understanding.

But confidence is not judgment.
Fluency is not responsibility.

This is not a moral failure. It is a human pattern — and a predictable one. Throughout history, when tools become powerful and useful, we begin to rely on them. Sometimes we mistake output for insight and efficiency for wisdom.

As humans and AI evolve together, our task is not to withdraw trust, but to deepen understanding — so that these tools expand human judgment rather than quietly replace it.

Artificial intelligence does not want anything. It does not care whether it is right for the right reasons. It does not feel the cost of being wrong. Those burdens still belong to us.

And yet, more often now, we allow machines to stand between us and the effort of thinking — not just about facts, but about values. About tradeoffs. About consequences.

This is where fear enters the conversation. Not the loud, cinematic fear of rebellion or apocalypse, but the quieter fear of erosion. The slow fading of judgment through disuse. The subtle comfort of letting something else decide.

Some people respond by rejecting AI outright. Others dismiss the concern entirely. Most of us live somewhere in between — alternating between fascination and unease depending on the day.

Yes.
No.
Maybe.

This book does not ask you to choose a side. It asks you to notice when you are choosing not to choose at all.

Tools have always changed us. What matters is not the tool, but how we choose to use it.

It can begin quietly.
Asking an AI to summarize an article instead of reading it.
Requesting a recommendation instead of comparing options.

Accepting a confident answer instead of pausing to question it.
None of these choices are wrong. Together, they illustrate how easily thinking can shift from practice to convenience.

The future will not be decided by machines becoming more intelligent. It will be decided by humans deciding how much thinking they are willing to keep.

It is an opportunity.

And that question is still ours to answer.

In the end, the advantage is simple:

Understanding + Intentional Use = Human Advantage

Chapter 2: When Power Arrives Faster Than Wisdom

Most technologies grow slowly enough for society to argue with them.

Artificial intelligence did not.

Within a remarkably short span of time, systems that once performed narrow, technical tasks began producing outputs indistinguishable from human work. They wrote passable prose, summarized complex material, recognized faces, translated languages, predicted behavior, and recommended actions. In some cases, they did these things better than humans under time pressure.

What arrived was not merely capability, but scale.

Machine learning systems thrive on volume. The more data they ingest, the more patterns they detect. Deep learning models amplify this effect, stacking layers of abstraction until relationships emerge that no individual could articulate. These systems do not reason as humans do, but they can approximate the results of reasoning well enough to be persuasive.

This is where unease begins — not because the systems are intelligent, but because they are confident.

A model trained on millions or billions of examples does not hesitate. It produces an answer even when uncertainty would be appropriate. It offers a conclusion even when the question itself is flawed. In human terms, it behaves like someone who has never learned to say, "I don't know."

That behavior would be concerning in a person. In a machine, it is often praised as efficiency.

The fear many people feel around artificial intelligence is not fear of replacement in the abstract. It is fear of authority without understanding. When outputs arrive fully formed — supported by statistics, probabilities, and technical language — they invite deference. Over time, deference becomes habit.

This dynamic is especially visible in systems that handle language and perception.

Natural language models speak fluently, creating the impression of comprehension. Computer vision systems see at scale, creating the impression of objectivity. Yet both share the same limitations: bias in data, gaps in context, and an absence of situational awareness. They do not know when they are wrong. They only know how often they have been right before. Being right is a matter of statistical weighting.

Which means the responsibility for judgment has not disappeared — it has shifted.
It now sits more visibly, and more deliberately, with us.

The problem is not error. Error is inevitable.

The problem is opacity.

As models grow more complex, their internal logic may become harder to interpret — even for the people who built them. Decisions emerge from layers of computation that cannot easily be explained after the fact. This creates a gap between output and accountability. When something goes wrong, responsibility becomes diffuse: the data, the model, the system, the user.

In that diffusion, human judgment quietly retreats.

This is not a failure of intelligence. It is a failure of pacing.

The accumulation of wisdom is slow. It accumulates through experience, reflection, disagreement, and consequence. It requires time to notice patterns — and humility to revise them. Artificial intelligence compresses capability without compressing judgment. It sometimes delivers answers faster than societies can decide how those answers should be used.

History offers many examples of this imbalance. Tools that scaled faster than norms created apparent instability before equilibrium returned. The difference now is speed — and reach. A flawed decision once affected, a person, a room, a factory, or a city. Today it can affect millions simultaneously.

That reality makes fear understandable.

Not dramatic fear. Not cinematic fear. But a quieter concern: that we may grant authority before we have agreed on responsibility.

Artificial intelligence did not create this risk.

It exposed it.

And it did so by doing exactly what we asked: processing more information than any human could, faster than any human should be expected to.

The challenge is not to slow intelligence. It is to ensure that judgment keeps pace.

That work remains stubbornly human.

Chapter 3: Automation Without Understanding

Automation has always promised relief.
Relief from repetition.
Relief from error.
Relief from the slow, imperfect work of human judgment.

As the world and its populations grew, the demand for goods and services grew with them.

Artificial intelligence fulfills that promise more convincingly than any tool before it. It does not merely automate physical labor or simple calculation; it automates decisions — or, more precisely, the appearance of decision-making. Systems classify, rank, approve, deny, recommend, and flag with remarkable speed. In many contexts, they do so better than hurried or distracted humans.

The danger lies not in automation itself, but in what quietly disappears alongside it.

Understanding.

Machine learning systems learn correlations, not causes. They identify patterns that *worked before* and apply them to what comes next. This is enormously useful — and fundamentally limited. A model does not know *why* a pattern exists. It does not know when circumstances have changed in ways the data cannot capture. It does not know when the cost of being wrong is unacceptable.

Humans usually do.

At least, we do when we are paying attention.

As automated systems improve, they reduce friction. Decisions arrive faster. Processes feel smoother. The absence of obvious failure becomes evidence of success. Over time, the human role shifts from decision-maker to overseer, and then — quietly — to rubber stamp.

This shift is rarely intentional.
It happens because automation works *most of the time.*

Consider systems used in hiring, lending, medical triage, content moderation, or security screening. These tools are introduced to manage scale, not to replace responsibility. Yet once embedded, they begin shaping outcomes long before a human intervenes. By the time a decision reaches review, the path has already been narrowed.

Automation, in this sense, does not remove humans from the loop.
It constrains the loop.

The result is a subtle inversion: humans no longer decide freely and use machines to assist; machines decide provisionally, and humans are asked to confirm. Over time, confirmation becomes routine. Routine becomes trust. Trust becomes dependence.

When something goes wrong, the explanation often sounds reasonable: the data was incomplete, the model behaved as expected, the threshold was set correctly. These explanations are technically accurate and ethically insufficient.

Understanding is not the same as explanation after the fact.

A human who understands a decision can challenge it before harm occurs. A system that optimizes outcomes cannot recognize when optimization itself may be the problem. Reinforcement-based systems, in particular, excel at maximizing reward functions — even when those rewards may not be fully aligned with human values. They learn what is measured, not what is meant.

This is not malicious behavior.
It is literal behavior.
It is algorithmic.
It is executing the code it was given.

Automation without understanding becomes most dangerous when it spreads quietly. No single failure triggers alarm. Instead, small misjudgments accumulate. Biases harden. Edge cases become policy. Exceptions disappear.

At that point, the system is no longer assisting human judgment.
It is shaping it.

There is a temptation to respond by demanding better models, more data, or tighter thresholds. Those improvements matter. But they do not resolve the underlying issue: understanding cannot be automated in the same way decisions can.

Understanding requires context, responsibility, and the ability to say, "This does not apply here."

Machines cannot say that on their own.

Humans can — but only if they remain engaged.

Automation should reduce unnecessary labor, not unnecessary thinking. When the latter disappears, efficiency begins to erode the very judgment it was meant to support.

The most important question, then, is not whether automated systems are accurate enough. It is whether the people who rely on them still understand what they are doing — and why.

If the answer becomes unclear, automation has succeeded technically and failed humanly.

To help us, early forms of AI mediator, restraint, apprentice, and oversight systems are already emerging across research and industry. Yet they remain fragmented and domain-specific. A fully integrated ecosystem of these roles has not yet arrived.

Chapter 4: The Illusion of Effortless Intelligence

Human beings are remarkably susceptible to fluency.

We tend to trust people who speak clearly, confidently, and without hesitation. We associate smooth language with competence, coherence, and understanding.

This is not irrational; for most of human history, fluency required effort, learning, and experience. Those who spoke well usually knew something worth hearing.

Artificial intelligence disrupts that assumption.

Modern language models generate text that is grammatically sound, stylistically flexible, and often persuasive. They summarize arguments, adopt tones, and respond conversationally. They do so without fatigue, uncertainty, or visible effort. The result is a new kind of output: language divorced from understanding, but convincingly intact.

This creates an illusion — not of intelligence,
but of *effortless* intelligence.

The danger here is subtle. People do not stop thinking because they are careless; they stop because thinking feels unnecessary. When a system produces a well-structured explanation in seconds, it tempts us to accept the result without interrogating the process. The friction that once signaled "this requires judgment" disappears.

Language-based systems are particularly powerful because they operate in the same medium humans use to reason with one another. They speak in sentences, not statistics. They explain, qualify, and reassure. In doing so, they blur the line between generating language and engaging in thought.

But language is not thought.
It is a vehicle for it.

A system trained to predict the next word based on vast amounts of text does not possess beliefs, intentions, or understanding. It does not know whether an argument is sound or whether a conclusion is ethical. It knows only which sequences of words tend to follow others. That this produces coherence is impressive. That it produces trust is more concerning.

This illusion is amplified by consistency. Unlike humans, machines do not hesitate. They do not pause to reconsider. They do not betray doubt unless explicitly instructed to simulate it. The absence of uncertainty reads as confidence, and confidence reads as authority.

Occasionally, the result is harmless. At other times, it is quietly consequential.

When language models are used to draft policies, generate reports, summarize evidence, or recommend actions, their fluency can mask gaps in reasoning. Errors may be subtle. Assumptions may go unchallenged. Context may be flattened. Yet because the output *sounds right*, it is treated as such.

The system did not mislead anyone. It performed exactly as designed.

The responsibility lies elsewhere.

Effortless intelligence is appealing because it relieves us of cognitive load. It allows us to move faster. It offers answers without struggle. But struggle has a purpose. It is how humans test ideas, notice inconsistencies, and develop judgment. Remove the struggle entirely, and the muscles of thinking begin to weaken.

This does not mean language-based AI should be avoided. It means it should be used deliberately. A fluent answer should invite scrutiny, not surrender. The smoother the output, the more important it becomes to ask what assumptions it rests upon — and whose responsibility it ultimately serves.

There is a quiet irony here. The more convincingly machines mimic human intelligence, the more essential distinctly human traits become: skepticism, reflection, and the willingness to pause.

Effortless intelligence is impressive.
Earned understanding remains indispensable.
Earned understanding is remembered.

Modern language models operate through mathematics — patterns, tokens, and probabilities predicting what words are likely to come next. The similarity to human recall can feel striking. But resemblance is not equivalence, and prediction is not understanding.

Beneath the fluency, the process remains mathematical.
And because of that, a confident answer feels complete.
It arrives quickly, clearly, and without hesitation.
Human expertise rarely feels that smooth — it includes uncertainty, caveats, and questions.
The contrast can be easy to miss.

Chapter 5: Ethics Without Ownership

Ethics fail most often where responsibility is unclear.

Artificial intelligence systems do not make moral choices. They execute instructions, optimize objectives, and follow patterns learned from data. When they produce harmful outcomes, the failure is rarely technical in isolation. It is ethical — and ethical failures require owners.

This is where unease sharpens.

As AI systems grow more capable, decision-making becomes distributed. A dataset is assembled by one group, a model by another, a system by a third, and deployment by a fourth. Each component may function as intended.

If mistakes occur, accountability can become diffuse.
Responsibility dissolves into process.

No one intended the outcome.
Everyone followed procedure.

Ethics cannot survive that environment.

Machine learning systems reflect the values embedded in their objectives, training data, and deployment context. Those values are often implicit, inherited rather than chosen. Optimization becomes a substitute for judgment. Metrics become proxies for meaning.

Reinforcement-based systems make this dynamic especially clear. They pursue rewards relentlessly, improving performance according to what is measured. When the reward function is poorly aligned — incomplete, short-sighted, or ethically thin — the system still succeeds. It simply succeeds at the wrong thing.

This is not a flaw in learning.
It is a flaw in intention.

Ethics require ownership because ethical decisions involve tradeoffs that cannot be optimized away. They demand judgment under uncertainty, accountability for consequences, and the willingness to accept blame when outcomes are wrong. Machines cannot do this. They cannot bear responsibility. They cannot answer for their decisions.

Humans can — but only if responsibility is not quietly delegated along with the task.

The most dangerous ethical failures in AI are rarely dramatic. They are procedural. A decision is automated because it saves time. Oversight is reduced because the system appears reliable. Human review is minimized because it slows progress. Each step feels reasonable. Together, they create systems that act without clear moral anchors.

At that point, ethics become aspirational rather than operational.

There is a temptation to respond with guidelines, principles, and compliance frameworks. These matter. But they are not sufficient. Ethics do not reside in documents. They reside in people who are empowered — and expected — to intervene.

An ethical system is not one that avoids error entirely.
It is one where someone remains answerable when errors occur.

Artificial intelligence makes it easy to obscure that answerability. It allows responsibility to be spread thin enough that no single actor feels compelled to stop the process, ask the uncomfortable question, or slow things down.

That is why ethics without ownership is not merely ineffective.
It is dangerous.

The question is not whether machines can act ethically. They cannot.
The question is whether humans will continue to do so when machines act on their behalf.

When ownership disappears, ethics soon follow.
Ethics require active human participation.

Chapter 6: Tools Have Always Changed Us

Every generation believes it is living through the most disruptive technological moment in history.

Sometimes it is right. Often it is simply close enough to feel that way.

Artificial intelligence is not the first tool to provoke anxiety about human relevance. Writing was once feared for weakening memory. Mechanical looms were blamed for eroding craftsmanship. Calculators were accused of destroying mathematical intuition. Each of these tools altered how humans worked, learned, and thought. None of them ended thinking. They changed *where* thinking occurred.

AI belongs to this tradition.

It emerged not because humans wished to stop thinking, but because thinking alone could no longer keep pace with the scale of the world. Data volumes expanded beyond individual comprehension. Systems became too complex for intuition alone. Decisions multiplied faster than attention. We built tools to cope.

This matters,
because it reframes the conversation.

If artificial intelligence were fundamentally alien to human effort, fear might be the appropriate response. But AI is deeply human in origin. It reflects our attempts to externalize pattern recognition, accelerate comparison, and reduce cognitive overload. It is a response to abundance, not to laziness.

The presence of risk does not negate this reality.

Tools have always redistributed effort. They move work from one domain to another. When calculators became common, arithmetic shifted from mental labor to conceptual understanding. When search engines emerged, recall gave way to navigation. Each transition demanded adaptation, not retreat.

The same is true here.

Used thoughtfully, AI can enhance human capability rather than diminish it. Machine learning systems can identify patterns and information clusters humans might never notice unaided. Computer vision can detect anomalies invisible to the naked eye. Language models can synthesize information faster than any single reader could manage. These are not trivial gains. In medicine, science, safety, and accessibility, they matter.

Fear that ignores these benefits becomes its own form of blindness.

The more productive question is not whether tools change us — they always do — but whether we understand *how* they change us. Change becomes dangerous when it is unconscious. When tools alter habits faster than we examine the consequences, judgment lags behind capability.

History shows that equilibrium eventually returns. New skills emerge. New norms form. Responsibility is renegotiated. What feels destabilizing at first becomes mundane. The printing press did not end thought; it changed literacy. The internet did not erase knowledge; it reorganized it.

Artificial intelligence will do the same.

The difference this time is speed. AI systems improve faster than institutions adapt. That mismatch creates anxiety. But anxiety alone is not a plan. Refusing to engage with powerful tools does not preserve judgment; it merely relinquishes influence to others who will use them anyway.

The choice is not between adoption and resistance.
It is between conscious use and passive drift.

Artificial intelligence does not absolve humans of responsibility. It magnifies the consequences of how responsibility is exercised. Used deliberately, it can support better decisions. Used carelessly, it can entrench poor ones at scale.

Tools have always changed us.
Throughout history, they have shaped human development—physically, cognitively, and socially.
What matters is whether we remain aware of the change while it is happening. Thinking, judgment, and active involvement remain essential.

Chapter 7: AI as Amplifier, Not Authority

Artificial intelligence is often described as intelligent.
This is convenient shorthand,
and frequently misleading.

What AI actually does — when it works — is amplify. It accelerates
pattern recognition, scales comparison, and extends human reach across
volumes of information no individual could process alone.

This is not a replacement for judgment. It is leverage.

Amplification does not create intelligence. It magnifies it. If human
thinking is careless, amplification spreads carelessness. If human thinking is
deliberate, amplification expands discovery.

Confusing leverage with authority is where problems begin.

Machine learning systems excel at identifying correlations across large
datasets. Deep learning models refine this ability, discovering structures
that are difficult for humans to articulate. Used appropriately, these
capabilities are transformative. They allow doctors to detect disease earlier,
engineers to optimize systems more efficiently, and scientists to explore
hypotheses that would otherwise remain hidden.

In these contexts,
AI does not decide.
It informs.

The distinction matters.

Authority implies responsibility. It implies accountability for consequences.
An authority can be questioned, challenged, and held to account. Artificial
intelligence systems cannot occupy that role. They are not designed to
understand goals, values, or tradeoffs. They operate within boundaries set
by others.

When AI is treated as an amplifier, humans remain responsible for
interpretation and action. When it is treated as an authority, responsibility
quietly shifts — often without acknowledgment.

This shift is rarely deliberate. It happens because amplification is impressive. When a system consistently improves outcomes, it earns trust. Over time, trust becomes reliance. Reliance becomes delegation. Delegation, when unexamined, becomes abdication.

The most effective AI deployments resist this progression by design. They embed friction. They require human confirmation. They surface uncertainty rather than conceal it. They remind users that outputs are suggestions, not verdicts.

These design choices are not technical constraints. They are ethical ones.

Treating AI as authority also creates a false sense of objectivity. Outputs feel neutral because they are produced by machines. In reality, they reflect human decisions made earlier: what data to include, what to measure, what to optimize, what to ignore. Authority without visibility becomes persuasion without consent.

Amplification, by contrast, preserves agency. It supports human reasoning rather than replacing it. It allows people to see more — not to decide less.

This is where optimism about AI is justified.

When used as a tool, artificial intelligence can raise the quality of decisions. It can highlight patterns, reveal blind spots, and reduce noise. It can free human attention for the kinds of thinking machines cannot perform: contextual judgment, moral reasoning, and purpose-driven choice.

The danger is not amplification itself.
The danger is forgetting who holds authority once amplification becomes routine.

Artificial intelligence should make us more capable — not less accountable.

AI will continue to evolve.
Its speed will increase.
Its fluency will improve.

What must not diminish is our willingness to think.
Because thinking is not automatic.
It is chosen.
And AI amplifies what we choose.

Using AI with purpose is powerful and valuable. Judgment is essential. Often restraint is too. That decision remains human.

Some things must remain human:
Thinking.
Participation.
Responsibility.
Accountability.
Ownership.
Purpose.
Judgment.

Chapter 8: Where Humans Still Matter More Than Ever

Predictions about artificial intelligence often focus on what machines will soon be able to do.

They list tasks, professions, and skills at risk. They chart curves of capability and speculate about timelines. What they rarely examine with the same rigor is what remains stubbornly human — not because machines are limited, but because responsibility cannot be automated.

This is where perspective matters.

Artificial intelligence excels in environments where goals are clear, data is abundant, and success can be measured. It struggles — by design — where ambiguity, values, and competing priorities collide.

These are not edge cases.

They describe most meaningful human decisions.

Consider medicine. AI systems can detect patterns in imaging data with remarkable accuracy. They can flag anomalies and suggest diagnoses. But deciding *what to do next* still requires human judgment: weighing risks, considering patient values, interpreting incomplete information, and communicating uncertainty. A model may identify a possibility. A physician must decide whether to act.

The same pattern appears elsewhere.

In law, AI can surface precedents but cannot determine justice.
In finance, it can optimize portfolios but cannot define fairness.

In education, it can personalize content but cannot decide what should matter.

These domains require more than prediction.
They require purpose.

Human value does not disappear as tools improve. It concentrates.

As machines take over repetitive and pattern-based tasks, human effort shifts toward interpretation, accountability, and meaning-making. This is not a demotion.

It is a narrowing of responsibility toward what only humans can do.

Ironically, this concentration can feel like loss. When tasks that once defined competence are automated, identity is unsettled. But competence was never the same as judgment. Skill was never the same as responsibility. What feels like erosion is often reallocation.

This is not automatic.
It requires intention.

Organizations that deploy AI without redefining human roles risk hollowing them out. Humans become supervisors without authority, reviewers without context, or decision-makers without ownership. In these environments, frustration grows — not because machines are capable, but because humans are underutilized.

The alternative is more demanding.

When AI is introduced thoughtfully, human roles are redesigned around accountability. People are empowered to question outputs, override recommendations, and slow processes when needed.
They are expected not merely to monitor systems, but to *own outcomes*.

This is harder than automation.
It requires trust in people as well as tools.

There is a temptation to assume that as machines become more capable, humans become less necessary. The opposite is often true. As systems scale, the cost of poor judgment increases. The need for responsible oversight grows, not shrinks.

The irony is unavoidable:
the more powerful artificial intelligence becomes, the more it exposes the importance of human purpose.

Machines can optimize.
Humans must decide what is worth optimizing.

Machines can act quickly.
Humans must decide when not to act.

Machines can suggest.
Humans must choose.

This is not a comforting conclusion for those hoping AI will relieve us of responsibility.
It is, however, a realistic one.

Artificial intelligence changes where humans matter — not whether they do.

Chapter 9: Creativity, Medicine, and the Good Kind of Leverage

Not all leverage is dangerous.

Some leverage expands human possibility without eroding judgment. It reduces friction where friction adds little value, and preserves resistance where resistance matters. Artificial intelligence, when used well, belongs in this category.

The clearest examples appear in domains where complexity overwhelms individual capacity.

In medicine, AI systems can analyze medical images, genomic data, and patient histories at scales no clinician could manage alone. They can surface rare conditions, identify subtle changes over time, and suggest avenues for investigation. These capabilities do not replace physicians; they extend them. They make it possible to see more, earlier, and with greater consistency.

The critical distinction is that these systems *inform* rather than decide.

A diagnosis is not a prediction. It is a judgment made under uncertainty, informed by evidence, experience, and patient context. AI can strengthen the evidence. It cannot assume responsibility for the judgment. When this boundary is respected, leverage improves care rather than compromising it.

Creativity offers a parallel case.

Generative systems can produce drafts, variations, and combinations at extraordinary speed. They can help writers explore ideas, designers iterate concepts, and artists experiment with form. Used thoughtfully, this accelerates exploration without dictating outcomes.

The human remains the editor, the curator, the final arbiter of meaning.

Problems arise when generation is mistaken for creation.

Creativity is not the act of producing options. It is the act of choosing among them — and knowing why. AI can expand the space of possibilities. It cannot determine which ones matter. When creators abdicate that choice, output multiplies while meaning thins.

The same pattern appears in science, engineering, and policy. AI can model scenarios, test assumptions, and reveal tradeoffs. It can expose blind spots and challenge intuition. These are benefits worth preserving. They depend, however, on humans remaining engaged at the point of decision.

This is the good kind of leverage: systems that amplify human effort without displacing human responsibility.

Such leverage is not accidental.
It is designed.

It requires clarity about roles. It requires explicit boundaries between suggestion and decision. It requires environments where questioning AI outputs is expected, not discouraged. Above all, it requires organizations to value judgment over speed — even when speed is available.

The temptation to push further is always present. If a system works well in an advisory role, why not grant it more autonomy? If errors are rare, why not remove friction? These questions are understandable. They are also dangerous when asked without reflection.

Leverage becomes liability when it obscures accountability.

The most successful uses of AI do not aim to eliminate humans from the process. They aim to elevate the parts of the process where humans add the most value. This is not nostalgia. It is pragmatism.

Artificial intelligence excels at pattern.
Humans excel at purpose.

When those strengths are aligned, leverage serves progress rather than replacing it.

New opportunities become available.

Chapter 10: The Difference Between Assistance and Abdication

Assistance preserves agency.
Abdication erodes it.

The line between the two is not always obvious, especially when systems perform well. Artificial intelligence often enters human workflows as a helper — a way to save time, reduce error, or manage complexity. The intent is rarely to surrender judgment. Yet over time, intention gives way to habit, and habit reshapes responsibility.

This is where clarity matters.

Assistance supports human decision-making without displacing it. It provides information, highlights options, and surfaces patterns. The human remains responsible for interpretation, context, and consequence.

Abdication, by contrast, occurs when the presence of a capable system quietly relieves humans of the obligation to decide.

The transition is subtle.

At first, a system offers recommendations.
Then those recommendations become defaults.
Eventually, deviation requires justification.

What began as support becomes authority — not because anyone decided it should, but because it was convenient.

This pattern appears across domains. In organizations, automated systems suggest actions that managers approve reflexively. In institutions, models rank risks that policymakers accept without challenge. In everyday life, people accept outputs because questioning them feels inefficient. None of this requires malice or negligence. It requires only trust unaccompanied by reflection.

The danger of abdication is not that machines make mistakes. It is that humans stop noticing when judgment is required.

Assistance assumes a thinking user.
Abdication assumes a passive one.

Design plays a role here, but culture plays a larger one. Systems that encourage questioning, expose uncertainty, and preserve friction tend to support assistance. Systems that hide assumptions, reward speed, and penalize deviation encourage abdication. The difference lies less in technology than in expectation.

Humans are highly adaptive. When tools remove the need to think, thinking atrophies. When tools require engagement, thinking deepens. This is not a flaw in human nature. It is how learning works.

There is a quiet irony in some AI deployments: the more reliable a system becomes, the more tempting it is to disengage.
Reliability breeds trust. Trust breeds complacency.
Complacency breeds dependence.

At that point, abdication no longer feels like a choice.
It feels like efficiency.

This is why optimism about AI must be paired with discipline. Assistance should reduce unnecessary effort, not unnecessary responsibility. The moment a system becomes the de facto decision-maker, humans lose more than time — they lose ownership.

Artificial intelligence does not demand abdication.
Humans offer it.

The distinction between the two is one of the most important questions of the AI age. It determines whether tools expand human capability or quietly replace the habits that sustain it.

Assistance asks: *What should I consider?*
Abdication asks: *What should I accept?*
Only one of those questions keeps humans fully engaged.
Thinking must remain actively engaged.

Chapter 11: Delegation vs. Dependency

Delegation is a sign of maturity.
Dependency is a sign of erosion.

The difference between the two is not technology. It is intent.

Delegation occurs when humans assign tasks while retaining responsibility for outcomes. It assumes oversight, understanding, and the ability to intervene.

Dependency emerges when tasks are handed over along with judgment, and responsibility quietly dissolves into process.

Artificial intelligence makes this distinction harder to see.

Because AI systems perform cognitive tasks — not just physical ones — delegation can look identical to dependency from the outside. A system generates a recommendation. A human approves it. Work proceeds. The surface behavior is the same. The underlying posture is not.

Delegation requires that humans remain capable of doing the task they delegate, at least in principle. Dependency does not. Over time, dependency reduces capability. Skills atrophy. Judgment dulls. Intervention becomes difficult because understanding has faded.

This is not hypothetical.
It is observable.

When people rely on navigation systems without occasionally reorienting themselves, spatial awareness declines. When professionals accept automated assessments without reviewing the reasoning, domain expertise weakens. When organizations depend on models without revisiting assumptions, strategy ossifies.

Artificial intelligence accelerates these effects because it operates at cognitive speed. Decisions are not merely assisted; they are pre-structured. The human role shifts from active reasoning to confirmation, then to oversight, and finally to exception handling. Each step feels efficient. Each step increases dependency.

The challenge is not to avoid delegation. It is to delegate without surrendering purpose.

Purpose differentiates intentional delegation from passive reliance. It answers the simple question: *Why is this task being delegated, and what remains human afterward?*
Without a clear answer, delegation drifts toward dependency.

This is where many AI users falter. Tasks are automated because they can be, not because it serves a coherent human goal. Efficiency becomes the default justification. Over time, efficiency replaces intention. The system runs smoothly, and no one asks what it is for.

Dependency thrives in that silence.

Reinforcement-based systems illustrate this danger. They adapt through feedback loops, optimizing behavior in response to rewards. When humans disengage from defining and revisiting those rewards, systems continue to improve — just not necessarily in the direction anyone intended. The system remains aligned with its objective. Humans lose alignment with their purpose.

Delegation, done well, resists this drift. It preserves friction where judgment matters. It demands periodic re-engagement. It treats AI outputs as provisional rather than authoritative. Most importantly, it insists that humans remain accountable for decisions — even when machines perform the work.

Dependency, by contrast, feels comfortable. It reduces effort and removes responsibility gradually enough that loss goes unnoticed. By the time intervention is needed, the capacity to intervene has weakened.

This is why the question of AI in society is not fundamentally about intelligence.
It is about **purpose**.

Delegation asks: *What are we trying to achieve, and why?*
Dependency forgets to ask.

Artificial intelligence can support human purpose, but it cannot supply one.

When purpose is absent, systems optimize blindly.
When purpose is present, delegation remains intentional.

The future of AI will be shaped less by what machines can do than by how deliberately humans choose to use them.
It will be defined by collaboration, not replacement.

That choice begins with knowing the difference between delegation and dependency — and refusing to confuse convenience with wisdom.

Chapter 12: Thinking Is a Muscle

Thinking weakens when it is not used.

This is not a metaphor. It describes how humans learn, adapt, and maintain judgment. Skills that are exercised strengthen. Skills that are outsourced decay. Artificial intelligence does not change this dynamic. It accelerates it.

For much of human history, thinking was unavoidable. Decisions required effort. Information was scarce. Errors were costly and visible. Judgment developed because it had to. Today, cognitive effort can be bypassed with ease. Answers arrive instantly. Explanations appear fully formed. Options are ranked before we ask how they were chosen.

The result is not ignorance.
It is passivity.

When thinking is treated as an inconvenience rather than a responsibility, it gradually loses strength. People become adept at selecting from options rather than generating them. Evaluation replaces reasoning. Approval replaces ownership.
Over time, independent thinking becomes less practiced — and therefore less reliable.

Artificial intelligence makes this dynamic tempting because it reduces friction so effectively. It does not demand struggle. It offers fluency, speed, and confidence. These qualities feel like progress. In many contexts, they are. But they come with a tradeoff: effort is no longer required to reach a conclusion.

Effort matters.

Struggle is not an inefficiency in human cognition; it is how judgment forms. It is how people notice contradictions, question assumptions, and develop perspective. When systems remove that struggle entirely, they also remove opportunities for growth, discovery, and new ideas.

This is where **purpose** becomes essential.

Purpose determines when effort is worth preserving. It answers the question: *What kinds of thinking do we want humans to keep doing?* Without an answer, efficiency becomes the default value. Everything that can be automated eventually will be — including the thinking that gives decisions meaning.

Purpose resists that drift.

A society with purpose does not ask only what machines can do. It asks what humans should continue to do, even when machines are capable. It protects certain forms of effort not because they are efficient, but because they are formative.

Education offers a clear example. AI systems can generate essays, solve problems, and explain concepts instantly. Used thoughtfully, they can support learning. Used indiscriminately, they replace it. The difference lies not in the technology, but in whether learning remains the goal.

The same is true in professional life. When AI systems prepare analyses, summarize evidence, and propose actions, humans must decide whether their role is to accept or to understand. Understanding takes time. It requires engagement. It cannot be automated.

Thinking, like muscle,
responds to demand.

If demand disappears, capacity follows. This does not happen all at once. It happens quietly, through convenience. Over time, people become less confident in their own judgment, not because it is inferior, but because it is unused. Deference feels safer than decision. Confirmation feels easier than challenge.

Artificial intelligence does not cause this outcome. It reveals a choice.

Purpose allows us to choose differently. It draws boundaries around what we delegate and what we retain. It insists that certain decisions remain human, not because machines are incapable, but because humans are meant to be accountable.

A future shaped only by efficiency would be fast and shallow. A future shaped by purpose preserves depth — even when speed is available.

Thinking is not an obstacle to progress.
It is the condition that makes progress worth pursuing.

The question is not whether AI will continue to improve. It will.
The question is whether humans will continue to think — deliberately,
responsibly, and with purpose — as they decide how to use it.
That question cannot be answered by a machine.

Thinking is not literally a muscle.
But it strengthens with use — and weakens with neglect.

Chapter 13: Ethics Are Not Optional Features

Ethics are often treated as accessories.

They appear late in the design process, framed as safeguards rather than foundations. They are documented, reviewed, and referenced — sometimes sincerely, sometimes ceremonially.

In technical systems, ethics are frequently positioned as constraints — limits placed on what a system may do after its capabilities are already defined.

This framing is backward.

Ethics are not features that can be added after intelligence is built. They are the conditions under which intelligence should be used. When they are treated as optional, they become fragile. When they are embedded from the start, they shape behavior.

Artificial intelligence makes this distinction unavoidable.

Unlike traditional tools, AI systems do not merely execute instructions. They adapt. They generalize. They act in ways that were not explicitly programmed. This adaptability is their strength — and the source of their ethical risk. A system that can operate beyond its creators' foresight must be governed by more than technical specifications.

It must be governed by intent.

Ethical intent cannot be inferred from data alone. Datasets reflect past behavior, not future values. They encode historical patterns, including inequities, blind spots, and assumptions that were never meant to be universal. Training a system on such data without ethical deliberation does not produce neutrality. It produces scale.

This is why ethics cannot be deferred.

When a system is optimized for efficiency, accuracy, or engagement without explicit ethical boundaries, it will pursue those goals relentlessly. Reinforcement learning makes this especially clear. A system rewarded for a measurable outcome will maximize that outcome — even if doing so undermines trust, fairness, or well-being. The system does not misbehave. It behaves exactly as instructed.

The ethical failure lies upstream.

Ethics require humans to define not only what is possible, but what is acceptable. They demand choices among competing goods, tolerance for ambiguity, and a willingness to accept responsibility when outcomes are imperfect. These are not computational problems. They are human ones.

This is where purpose re-enters the conversation.

Purpose provides the context in which ethical decisions make sense. It answers why a system exists, whom it serves, and what tradeoffs are justified. Without purpose, ethics become abstract principles disconnected from action. With purpose, they become operational constraints.

Regulatory frameworks emerge from this need. They are not expressions of fear, but of collective judgment. Regulations attempt to formalize ethical boundaries at a societal level, insisting on transparency, accountability, and human oversight.
They recognize a simple truth: when systems scale, so do consequences.

Yet regulation alone is not enough.

No framework can anticipate every context. No guideline can replace individual judgment. Ethics ultimately depend on people who are empowered — and expected — to intervene. A system may comply with every rule and still produce harm if no one feels responsible for questioning it.

This is the risk of procedural ethics: everything is followed, and no one thinks.

Ethical use of artificial intelligence requires more than compliance. It requires a culture that values judgment over speed, reflection over automation, and responsibility over convenience. It requires humans who understand not only how systems work, but why they are used.

Ethics are not obstacles to innovation. They prevent innovation from drifting into harm. They slow processes when slowing is necessary. They introduce friction where friction protects what matters.

Artificial intelligence does not make ethics obsolete. It makes them unavoidable.

When ethics are treated as optional, intelligence becomes dangerous. When they are treated as foundational, intelligence becomes valuable.

The difference lies not in technology, but in purpose — and in the humans willing to uphold it.

Chapter 14: Who Is Accountable When No One Is Thinking?

Accountability fails quietly.

It rarely collapses in a single moment. More often, it thins out over time, distributed across systems, teams, processes, and policies until no one feels fully responsible. Artificial intelligence accelerates this diffusion, not because it intends to, but because it makes delegation easier than reflection.

When something goes wrong in an AI-enabled system, the question of responsibility becomes complicated very quickly. Was it the data? The model? The design choice? The deployment context? The user who approved the recommendation? The organization that set the incentives?

Each answer contains some truth.
None of them feel complete.

This fragmentation is not accidental. It is structural. AI systems are built and deployed by networks of people rather than single decision-makers. Responsibility is shared, but accountability often is not. In that gap, ethical clarity erodes.

The problem becomes most visible when no one feels authorized to intervene.

Eventually, thinking stops.

A system produces an output that feels wrong, but also feels supported by metrics. A human notices discomfort, but lacks the confidence or authority to challenge the process. Over time, discomfort is suppressed in favor of efficiency. Questioning slows things down. Silence keeps things moving.

This is not a failure of courage. It is a failure of design and expectation. Systems that prioritize speed, scale, and consistency discourage interruption. Human judgment becomes an exception rather than a norm. Accountability shifts from individuals to workflows.

Yet accountability cannot live in workflows alone.

To be accountable is to be answerable — not only to outcomes, but to reasons. It requires someone who can say, "This decision was mine," and accept the consequences that follow. Machines cannot do this. Committees struggle to do it. Processes are not designed to do it.

Only people can.

Artificial intelligence complicates accountability because it obscures causality. When decisions emerge from layers of computation, tracing influence becomes difficult. Technical opacity is often mistaken for moral ambiguity. But difficulty does not eliminate responsibility. It only makes the need for clarity more urgent.

Accountability must be designed deliberately.

That design includes clear ownership of decisions, explicit authority to override systems, and cultural permission to slow processes when something feels wrong. It also includes education — not only in how systems function, but in what they are for. People cannot be accountable for decisions they do not understand or feel empowered to question.

This is where purpose again plays a central role.

Purpose anchors accountability. It provides a reference point when metrics conflict, when incentives pull in different directions, and when efficiency pressures mount. Without purpose, accountability becomes procedural. With purpose, it becomes personal.

A society that delegates decisions without preserving accountability risks more than error. It risks moral numbness. When no one is thinking, no one feels responsible. When no one feels responsible, harm becomes systemic rather than accidental.

Artificial intelligence does not absolve humans of accountability.
It concentrates it.

As systems grow more powerful, the cost of unowned decisions increases. The need for humans who are willing to think, question, and take responsibility becomes more acute — not less.

The question is not whether accountability can be automated.
It cannot.
The question is whether humans will insist on retaining it.

That insistence is not technological.
It is ethical.
And it is purposeful.

Chapter 15: Raising Humans in an AI World

Every technology eventually reshapes what it means to grow up.

Children raised after the printing press encountered books as ordinary objects. Those raised after electricity assumed light on demand. The internet normalized instant access to information. Artificial intelligence will shape a generation for whom answers are available — and effort can feel optional.

This is neither dystopian nor utopian.
It is simply consequential.

The question is not whether children should use AI. They will. The question is what kind of humans they become while doing so. Education has always been about more than information transfer. It is about forming judgment, curiosity, resilience, and the capacity to think independently.

AI challenges these goals not by opposing them, but by making shortcuts irresistibly easy.

When a system can write an essay, solve a problem, or explain a concept instantly, the temptation is to measure success by output rather than understanding. Learning becomes performance. Curiosity becomes optional. The struggle that once shaped thinking is quietly removed.

This does not mean AI has no place in education.

It means its place must be intentional.

Used thoughtfully, AI can support exploration, personalize learning, and expand access. It can help students see connections, test ideas, and receive feedback faster than traditional systems allow. But it cannot replace the formative experience of wrestling with uncertainty.

Children learn how to think by thinking.

If AI consistently stands between students and effort, it changes what competence feels like. Confidence becomes external. Judgment is borrowed. Over time, the habit of asking *why* weakens, replaced by asking, *What does the system say?*

Raising humans in an AI world requires preserving certain kinds of friction. Not because friction is virtuous, but because it is formative. Just as physical development requires resistance, cognitive development requires challenge.

Adults face the same risk.

Professionals who rely exclusively on AI-generated analysis may produce more work, faster. They may also lose the ability to recognize when that work is flawed. Over time, confidence shifts from internal judgment to external validation. Expertise becomes procedural rather than conceptual.

This is not a failure of individuals.
It is a design problem.

A society that values speed above understanding will raise citizens optimized for compliance rather than judgment. A society that values purpose will teach people when to slow down, question outputs, and take responsibility for decisions.

The goal is not to raise humans who compete with machines.
It is to raise humans who know when not to rely on them and when to use them.

Artificial intelligence can support learning.
It cannot replace formation.

What we choose to preserve — effort, reflection, curiosity — will shape not only how AI is used, but who we become alongside it.

Chapter 16: Using AI Without Losing Yourself

The most difficult questions about artificial intelligence are not technical. They are personal.

They arise not in policy debates or design meetings, but in quiet moments of use: when an answer appears instantly, when effort can be skipped, when judgment can be deferred. These moments feel small. Taken together, they shape habits. Habits shape identity.

Using AI without losing yourself begins with noticing those moments.

The distinction is subtle but decisive. A tool can answer for you, or it can think with you. The difference lies not in the machine, but in whether you remain actively engaged in the process of reasoning.

Artificial intelligence is at its most seductive when it removes friction. It offers clarity where there was uncertainty, speed where there was delay, and confidence where there was hesitation. None of this is inherently harmful.

The risk emerges when convenience becomes default and default becomes dependence.

The difference is rarely obvious in the moment.

A person who consults an AI system to explore an idea may deepen understanding. A person who consults it to avoid thinking may slowly disengage. The action looks the same. The intent does not.

This is why purpose matters at the individual level as much as at the societal one.

Purpose asks: *What am I using this tool for, and what am I choosing to retain?* Without that question, use becomes reactive. With it, use becomes deliberate.

There are decisions we make not because machines are incapable, but because making them shapes who we are. Choosing words carefully develops clarity. Working through a problem builds intuition. Arguing with oneself refines judgment. When these activities are bypassed consistently, something is lost — not productivity, but agency.

Using AI well requires restraint.

Restraint does not mean avoidance. It means choosing where to engage fully and where to delegate. It means recognizing that some forms of effort are worth preserving even when shortcuts are available. It means accepting that speed is not always the highest value.

This posture can feel inefficient. It is.

That inefficiency is the point.

A person capable of independent thought is not one who never uses tools, but one who knows when not to. They are willing to pause, to question an output, to revise it — or to reject it entirely. They treat AI-generated answers as drafts, not verdicts.

This requires confidence in one's own judgment, which in turn requires practice.

There is a quiet paradox here.
The more powerful AI becomes, the more important it is for individuals to cultivate skills that are not easily automated: critical thinking, ethical reasoning, contextual awareness, and the ability to live with uncertainty. These are not nostalgic virtues.
They are practical ones.

Artificial intelligence can support decision-making. It cannot replace responsibility for decisions. When individuals forget this, they risk becoming intermediaries in their own lives — approving choices they did not fully understand.

Using AI without losing yourself means remaining the author of your decisions, even when machines help draft them.

It means asking not only whether an answer is correct, but whether it is *yours*.

Chapter 17: Designing Guardrails for Minds, Not Machines

When discussions turn to AI safety, they often focus on machines.

How do we constrain systems?
How do we limit capabilities?
How do we prevent misuse?

These are important questions.
They are also incomplete.

The most effective guardrails in any complex system are not built solely into the technology. They are built into the people who use it — their incentives, expectations, and willingness to intervene. Artificial intelligence is no exception.

In machine learning, guardrails take the form of training data selection, validation testing, monitoring, and human review. They are designed to detect errors, reduce bias, and limit unintended outcomes.

In humans, guardrails look different. They appear as judgment, skepticism, professional responsibility, and the willingness to pause when something feels wrong.

Purpose gives guardrails direction and focus.

Machines follow rules.
Humans decide when rules matter.

Designing guardrails for minds means acknowledging a simple truth: no technical safeguard can replace human judgment. Systems can be constrained, audited, and monitored, but they cannot recognize when a situation falls outside the assumptions under which they were built. Humans can — if they are encouraged to do so.

Large language models are trained on vast collections of human writing and speech. That material reflects the full range of human knowledge, creativity, bias, error, and disagreement.

We want intelligent AI. Intelligence, by definition, should improve clarity, judgment, and understanding. Systems that amplify bias or distortion are not demonstrating intelligence — they are reflecting unfiltered data.

This is where some AI deployments can falter. Guardrails do exist, and they matter. AI guardrails are technical, procedural, and policy-based controls designed to help systems operate within safe, ethical, and legal boundaries.

They filter inputs, monitor outputs, and aim to prevent biased, proprietary, or harmful information from being generated or released.

Yet even the best technical safeguards cannot replace human judgment.

Guardrails exist.
They help.
They are not sufficient alone.

Organizations often invest heavily in technical controls while neglecting cultural ones. They specify thresholds, validation checks, and monitoring dashboards, but fail to define when and how people are expected to override systems. Intervention becomes theoretically possible and practically discouraged.

Guardrails that are never used are ornamental.

Effective guardrails create friction deliberately. They slow decisions at critical points. They require justification rather than passive approval. They make uncertainty visible instead of smoothing it away. Most importantly, they assign responsibility explicitly, so people know when they are expected to think.

This approach can feel inefficient.
It is.
That inefficiency is a feature, not a flaw.

High-stakes decisions benefit from resistance. Friction forces reflection. It creates space for ethical reasoning and contextual awareness — capacities machines do not possess. Designing systems that remove all friction assumes speed is always desirable. Experience suggests otherwise.

Regulatory frameworks gesture toward this principle. Requirements for human oversight, explainability, and accountability exist not because machines are untrustworthy, but because humans are fallible — and must remain engaged.

Regulation attempts to encode collective judgment into process, insisting that certain decisions remain interruptible.

Yet guardrails cannot live in regulation alone.

They must be reinforced by organizational norms and individual behavior. People must feel authorized to question systems, to pause processes, and to bear responsibility for outcomes. Without that authorization, even the most thoughtful safeguards become hollow.

Designing guardrails for minds also means educating users. Understanding what a system can and cannot do is essential, but insufficient. Users must also understand *why* it exists, *what* it optimizes, and *whose* values it reflects. Without this context, oversight becomes mechanical rather than meaningful.

The goal is not to constrain intelligence, artificial or otherwise.
It is to preserve judgment under pressure.

Artificial intelligence magnifies the consequences of our design choices. Systems that encourage engagement produce thoughtful outcomes. Systems that reward speed and compliance produce efficient ones.

The difference is not technological.
It is intentional.

Guardrails that work do not remove responsibility.
They make responsibility unavoidable.

And that is precisely what a society living alongside powerful AI must insist upon.

Chapter 18: Choosing When Not to Ask the Machine

There will always be another answer available.

That may be one of the most profound changes artificial intelligence introduces into human life. For nearly every question, at nearly every moment, a response can be generated instantly — fluent, confident, and often persuasive. The scarcity that once forced judgment has largely disappeared.

What remains scarce is discretion.

Choosing when *not* to ask the machine is not an act of resistance. It is an act of authorship. It signals an understanding that not every question benefits from speed, and not every decision should be optimized.

Some questions require thinking before answering.
Some require responsibility before efficiency.
Some require silence before certainty.

Artificial intelligence is remarkably good at producing responses. It is not good at knowing which questions matter most to the person asking them. That discernment cannot be automated. It belongs to humans alone.

This does not mean AI should be avoided in moments of importance. It means it should be used with intention. The difference lies in posture. When people ask machines to replace effort, they narrow themselves. When they ask machines to *support* effort, they expand what is possible.

The most thoughtful users of AI develop a quiet discipline. They notice when they are tempted to outsource thinking prematurely. They recognize when a system's confidence exceeds their own understanding. They pause. They ask whether the question they are asking is the right one — or simply the easiest.

There is another choice we rarely notice: choosing not to ask at all. Not every question must be delegated to a machine, and when we do choose to ask, the purpose of the question matters.

Before asking AI, it is worth asking ourselves: *What am I trying to understand? What kind of answer would truly help?* That moment of reflection prepares us to interpret the response, question it, refine it, or ask again with greater clarity.

Context shapes every answer.
A question asked without purpose invites a shallow response.
A question asked with intention invites judgment.

Asking well is not a technical skill.
It is a thinking skill.

This discipline does not slow progress.

It refines it.

A society that retains the habit of choosing when not to ask the machine preserves something essential: the ability to live with uncertainty. Not all questions admit immediate answers. Not all decisions benefit from optimization. Wisdom often emerges from reflection, disagreement, and time.

Artificial intelligence cannot wait.
Humans can — and sometimes should.

Choosing not to ask the machine is also an ethical act.
It acknowledges that responsibility cannot be delegated entirely, even when delegation is possible. It affirms that judgment matters most where consequences are real and irreversible.

This choice will not always be popular.
Speed will be rewarded.
Efficiency will be praised.
Automation will be framed as progress.

In that environment, restraint can feel like hesitation.

It is not.

Restraint is clarity. It is the recognition that power requires boundaries, and that intelligence without purpose is directionless.
Choosing when not to ask the machine is how humans assert those boundaries — quietly, consistently, and without spectacle.

The question that opened this book remains.

Does AI scare you?

Perhaps it did at first. Perhaps it no longer does. Perhaps it never did. If your answer has shifted, that is not inconsistency. It is engagement.

Yes.
No.
Maybe.

These were never destinations. They were positions from which to think.

Artificial intelligence will continue to evolve.
Its capabilities will grow.
Its presence will deepen.
None of this absolves humans of responsibility.
If anything, it concentrates it.

The future will not be decided by what machines are capable of doing.
It will be decided by what humans choose to do — and choose not to do — alongside them.

The machine will always have an answer.

The thinking remains ours.
It requires participation.

Selection.
Intention.
Restraint.
Alignment.
Purpose.

Afterword: On Staying Human

Every generation inherits its tools and decides, often implicitly, what kind of people it will become while using them.

Artificial intelligence is the latest — and perhaps the most revealing — of those tools. It exposes our assumptions about efficiency, authority, and effort. It shows us how easily judgment can be delegated, and how quietly responsibility can fade when answers are always available.

This book has argued for neither fear nor surrender.
It has argued for attention.

Attention to where power accumulates.
Attention to where thinking weakens.
Attention to where purpose is required to keep intelligence from drifting.

Artificial intelligence did not remove human responsibility. It clarified it. In a world where machines can generate answers endlessly, choosing when to pause, question, or refrain becomes an act of intention.
That intention is not technical.
It is ethical.

Staying human does not mean rejecting tools. It means refusing to let tools decide who we are. It means preserving judgment where consequences matter, accepting uncertainty where certainty is premature, and choosing effort where effort shapes character.

The future will include more intelligent machines.
That outcome is already set in motion.
What remains open is whether humans will continue to think deliberately, act responsibly, and live with purpose alongside them.

That choice will not be made once.
It will be made daily, quietly, and without announcement.

And it will remain ours.

Appendix A: A Brief Map of Artificial Intelligence

This book deliberately avoided technical deep dives. Not because the technology is unimportant, but because understanding artificial intelligence begins with how it shapes human judgment, responsibility, and purpose.

True technical mastery requires the ability to read, write, and change code — and that level of depth, while valuable, is not necessary for engaging with the ethical and societal questions this book raises.

Still, readers often ask a practical question: *What do we actually mean by "AI"?*

This appendix offers a brief orientation — not as a manual, but as a map. It describes the major AI domains referenced throughout the book and explains why they matter socially and ethically. The descriptions are intentionally concise and future-proof.

Because this book is about responsibility, not implementation.

Machine Learning (ML)

Learning from patterns

Machine learning refers to systems that identify patterns in data and use those patterns to make predictions or classifications. Rather than following fixed rules, ML systems adapt based on examples.

Why it matters:
ML shifts decision-making from explicit logic to statistical inference. This enables scale, but also obscures reasoning. When predictions replace explanations, judgment must compensate.

Deep Learning & Neural Networks

Layered abstraction

Deep learning uses multi-layered neural networks to extract increasingly abstract representations from data. These systems power many modern breakthroughs in vision, language, and speech.

Why it matters:

As models grow more complex, interpretability declines. This increases performance while reducing transparency — intensifying the tension between accuracy and accountability.

Natural Language Processing (NLP)

Language without understanding

NLP systems process and generate human language. Modern language models produce fluent, context-sensitive text that often appears thoughtful or authoritative.

Why it matters:

Fluency creates trust. When language feels intelligent, humans may defer judgment too quickly. NLP systems amplify communication while separating language from intention.

Computer Vision (CV)

Perception at scale

Computer vision systems analyze images and video to identify objects, faces, patterns, and anomalies. They operate at speeds and scales far beyond human perception.

Why it matters:

CV systems are capable of interpreting visual data with speed, accuracy, and precision that often exceeds human capabilities. Errors in perception may become errors in policy when vision systems are embedded in surveillance, security, healthcare, or automated decision-making. Misclassification scales quickly. These systems are important for automating complex tasks, enhancing safety, and improving quality control in manufacturing, healthcare, autonomous driving, and security.

Reinforcement Learning (RL)

Optimization through reward

Reinforcement learning systems improve behavior by maximizing reward signals over time. They are particularly powerful in dynamic environments.

Why it matters:
RL systems pursue what is measured, not what is meant. Poorly defined rewards can produce unintended and ethically problematic outcomes, even when systems are technically successful. Proper coding is key. RL systems are an important frontier. These specialize in decision-making and optimal control through trial-and-error similar to human learning. Robotics, gaming, and strategy optimization are aspects of RL.

Robotics & Embodied AI

Intelligence in the physical world

Robotics combines AI with physical action. Embodied systems must navigate uncertainty, constraints, and real-world consequences.

Why it matters:
Physical environments impose limits that software alone does not. These limits slow autonomy and highlight accountability, making robotics a revealing test case for human oversight.

Agentic Systems

Delegated action

Agentic AI systems are designed to pursue goals, make decisions, and act with limited human intervention, often across multiple steps.

Why it matters:
Agentic systems intensify questions of delegation, dependency, and accountability. When systems act on behalf of humans, responsibility must be explicitly retained. Agentic systems are powerful because they go beyond generating content to autonomously executing multi-step workflows and making decisions. To achieve this they function as active agents and use designed reasoning, planning, and tool integration to achieve goals without constant human oversight.

Artificial General Intelligence (AGI)

A speculative horizon

AGI refers to hypothetical systems capable of broad, human-like reasoning across domains. No such systems currently exist.

Why it matters:

AGI debates often distract from present responsibilities. This book focuses on today's systems, where ethical choices are already real and consequential. The goal is to exhibit human-level cognitive abilities, so that they are enabled to learn, apply knowledge, and reason across multiple or any domains. AGI will need to adapt to new, unforeseen situations and learn from them mimicking human cognitive flexibility.

Artificial Superintelligence (ASI)

Beyond human cognitive capacity

Artificial Superintelligence refers to hypothetical systems that would exceed human intelligence across nearly all domains, including reasoning, planning, creativity, and strategic decision-making. Such systems do not currently exist and remain speculative.

Why it matters:

Discussions of ASI often dominate public imagination, but they risk obscuring more immediate concerns. The ethical challenges associated with superintelligence — alignment, control, and unintended consequences — are extensions of problems that already exist in narrower systems today.

Focusing exclusively on ASI can be a form of ethical deferral: concern is projected onto a distant future while present systems operate without sufficient oversight, purpose, or accountability.

If humanity struggles to govern limited intelligence responsibly, the challenge will not disappear with greater capability. It will intensify.

The question ASI ultimately raises is not whether machines might become too intelligent, but whether humans will develop the discipline, purpose, and governance structures required to remain responsible stewards of intelligence at any scale.

A Closing Note on Purpose

These domains differ technically, but they share a common risk: intelligence can scale faster than human reflection. None of these systems possess purpose. They inherit it — or lack it — from the people who design, deploy, and rely on them.

Understanding AI, then, is not primarily about mastering categories. It is about recognizing where judgment must remain human.

This appendix may expand in future editions. The responsibility it points to will not.

Appendix B: Tools, Transitions, and the Long Arc of Human Capability

Purpose

This appendix is not intended as a comprehensive history of technology. It is a contextual map. Throughout human history, tools have repeatedly shifted how work, knowledge, and responsibility are distributed.

Each major transition has altered what humans do directly, what they delegate, and what remains their responsibility. Artificial intelligence belongs to this long arc—not as an anomaly, but as the latest and most consequential redistribution of effort yet.

Tools and technologies, in their time, represent opportunities.

A Brief Chronology of Tools and Transitions

Era / Tool	Approx. Date	What Changed	Shift in Human Effort and Responsibility
Egyptian Hieroglyphics	c. 3200 BCE	Language externalized	Memory moved from individuals to records; responsibility shifted to interpretation and preservation
Phoenician Navigation & Maritime Trade	c. 1200–800 BCE	Long-distance trade scaled	Trust moved from personal familiarity to contracts, symbols, and navigation knowledge
Greek Alphabet & Philosophy	c. 800–400 BCE	Literacy broadened	Knowledge became shareable; responsibility shifted toward reasoning and debate
Roman Roads & Administration	c. 300 BCE–400 CE	Infrastructure standardized	Coordination scaled; responsibility shifted to governance and logistics
Manuscripts & Early Scholarly Institutions	c. 500–1400	Knowledge centralized	Authority concentrated; responsibility lay in stewardship and transmission

Era / Tool	Approx. Date	What Changed	Shift in Human Effort and Responsibility
Printing Press	c. 1450	Information democratized	Literacy expanded; responsibility shifted to discernment rather than access
Postal Systems & Pony Express	1600s–1860s	Communication accelerated	Time collapsed; responsibility shifted toward reliability and coordination
Telegraph	1830s–1850s	Instant long-distance communication	Decision-making sped up; responsibility increased for accuracy and timing
AC/DC Electrical Power	Late 1800s	Energy standardized	Physical labor redistributed; responsibility shifted to system safety and control
Assembly Lines	Early 1900s	Production mechanized	Skill fragmented; responsibility moved toward design and oversight
Global Shipping & Containerization	Mid-1900s	Trade globalized	Complexity abstracted; responsibility shifted to systems and regulation
Flight & Aerospace Engineering	1900s–1960s	Distance collapsed	Risk increased; responsibility became formalized and procedural
Slide Rule	1600s–1970s	Calculation accelerated	Mental arithmetic reduced; responsibility shifted to conceptual understanding
Electronic Calculators	1970s	Arithmetic automated	Computation delegated; responsibility moved to framing and checking
Mainframe & Personal Computers	1950s–1990s	Information processing scaled	Memory and logic externalized; responsibility shifted to programming and intent
Computer Programming	1960s–present	Instructions formalized	Precision required; responsibility lay in logic, design, and consequences

Era / Tool	Approx. Date	What Changed	Shift in Human Effort and Responsibility
Space Exploration	1950s–present	Human reach extended beyond Earth	Risk amplified; responsibility formalized through systems, ethics, and policy
Global Digital Infrastructure (Internet)	1990s–present	Knowledge reorganized	Access universalized; responsibility shifted to navigation and judgment
Artificial Intelligence	2000s–present	Pattern recognition automated	Cognitive effort redistributed; responsibility remains human

Interpretive Note

Across these transitions, a pattern emerges. Tools rarely eliminate human responsibility; they relocate it. As effort is offloaded, judgment becomes more important, not less. Each new capability demands a corresponding increase in clarity of purpose, ethical framing, and accountability. Artificial intelligence follows this pattern—but at a scale and speed that compresses adaptation time and magnifies consequences.

Ask: "What kind of thinking does this new tool demand from us?"

Selected Reading & Foundational Sources

Chosen for historical and conceptual context; not intended to be exhaustive.

Diamond, Jared.
Guns, Germs, and Steel: The Fates of Human Societies.
W. W. Norton & Company, 1997.
ISBN: **978-0393317558 (Pulitzer PrizeWinner, 1998)**

Ong, Walter J.
Orality and Literacy: The Technologizing of the Word.
Routledge, 1982.
ISBN: **978-0415538381**

Goody, Jack.
The Logic of Writing and the Organization of Society.

Cambridge University Press, 1986.
ISBN: **978-0521339629**

Mumford, Lewis.
Technics and Civilization.
University of Chicago Press, 1934 (reprint editions available).
ISBN: **978-0226550275**

Nye, David E.
Technology Matters: Questions to Live With.
MIT Press, 2006.
ISBN: **978-0262640643**

Ceruzzi, Paul E.
A History of Modern Computing.
MIT Press, 2nd Edition, 2003.
ISBN: **978-0262532030**

Floridi, Luciano.
The Ethics of Information.
Oxford University Press, 2013.
ISBN: **978-0199641321**

Headrick, Daniel R.
The Invisible Weapon: Telecommunications and International Politics, 1851–1945.
Oxford University Press, 1991.
ISBN: **978-0195070033**

Basalla, George.
The Evolution of Technology.
Cambridge University Press, 1988.
ISBN: **978-0521296816**

EU Medical Device Regulation (MDR) 2017/745
Official Journal of the European Union.
(Primary regulatory source; no ISBN)

U.S. Food and Drug Administration (FDA)
Clinical Decision Support Software Guidance
Software as a Medical Device (SaMD) Guidance
(Primary regulatory guidance documents; no ISBN)

About the Author

Mark Anderson, PhD works at the intersection of human judgment, technology, and responsibility. With a background spanning artificial intelligence, data science, regulatory strategy, and complex decision-making systems, his work focuses on how powerful tools shape — and sometimes limit — human thinking.

His experience includes applied machine learning, deep learning, and AI-enabled workflows across healthcare, science, and regulated environments, where ethical clarity and human oversight are not optional.

He believes AI, when guided by clear purpose, can help generate knowledge, improve decision-making, chart space, uncover ancient ruins, and expand what humans are able to discover and create.

Does AI Scare You? reflects that concern — not with what machines might become, but with what humans choose to remain.

Tools have always changed us. What matters is how we choose to use them.

Back-Cover Copy

DOES AI SCARE YOU?

Yes. No. Maybe.

Artificial intelligence is powerful. What matters is how we choose to use it — and what we allow it to replace.

As AI becomes faster and more fluent, it begins to shape decisions once made by humans: what we trust, what we prioritize, and how much thinking we delegate. The danger is not that machines will think like us — but that we may stop thinking deliberately at all.

In this calm and thoughtful exploration, **Mark Anderson, PhD** moves beyond fear and hype to ask a harder question: How do we use powerful tools without surrendering agency, purpose, or accountability?

If you already embrace AI, this book invites reflection.
If you distrust it, this book invites curiosity.
Most readers will finish somewhere in between.

Clear-eyed and quietly urgent, *Does AI Scare You?* is for anyone navigating a world where answers are easy — but thinking remains essential.

Thinking is active.
AI amplifies it.
Purpose directs it.

Book Description

Does AI Scare You? Yes. No. Maybe.

Artificial intelligence is rapidly moving from technical novelty to everyday presence. It writes, recommends, predicts, and increasingly influences decisions once made by humans. The real question is no longer whether AI will change the world—it already has. The deeper question is how it will change the way we think, decide, and take responsibility.

In this clear and thoughtful exploration, Mark Anderson, PhD moves beyond fear and hype to examine how AI reshapes human judgment, accountability, and purpose. Rather than focusing on speculative futures or technical instruction, the book asks what we choose to delegate to machines—and what we must deliberately retain.

Through accessible discussion of machine learning, natural language processing, computer vision, robotics, and emerging agentic systems, the book shows how powerful tools subtly influence habits of thought, institutions, and daily decision-making. It offers a balanced perspective that acknowledges real risks without surrendering to alarmism, and recognizes real benefits without abandoning human agency.

Does AI Scare You? invites readers to consider a third position between optimism and fear: intentional use. Written for professionals, educators, policymakers, and curious readers alike, this book is a calm, practical reflection on living and working in an era where answers are increasingly easy—but thinking remains essential.

Available Books by the Author

Speculative Fiction & Thoughtful Science

- *The Alignment Echo*
  A novel about whether intelligence is something that speaks—or something that knows when not to.

Children's & Bilingual Adventures

- *Tommi the Green Tomato* (series)
  Playful, imaginative stories about curiosity, friendship, and growing wiser—told with humor and heart.

Creative Cooking & Everyday Intelligence

- *The Accidental Genius & Snackcidents*
  Practical, inventive cooking that turns beans, grains, and real hunger into satisfying food—with curiosity baked in.

www.ingramcontent.com/pod-product-compliance
Lightning Source LLC
Chambersburg PA
CBHW050848260726
48660CB00006B/2503